T0052141

by Scott R. Welvaert
illustrated by Ron Frenz and
Charles Barnett III

Consultant:
Kristin Johnson, Librarian
Salt Lake Community College
Salt Lake City, Utah
Editor, *Unfortunate Emigrants: Narratives of the Donner Party*

Capstone press
Mankato, Minnesota

Graphic Library is published by Capstone Press,
1710 Roe Crest Drive, North Mankato, Minnesota 56003
www.capstonepub.com

Copyright © 2006 by Capstone Press, a Capstone imprint. All rights reserved.
No part of this publication may be reproduced in whole or in part, or stored in a retrieval system, or transmitted in any form or by any means, electronic, mechanical, photocopying, recording, or otherwise, without written permission of the publisher.
For information regarding permission, write to Capstone Press,
1710 Roe Crest Drive, North Mankato, Minnesota 56003

Library of Congress Cataloging-in-Publication Data
Welvaert, Scott R.
The Donner Party / by Scott Welvaert; illustrated by Ron Frenz and Charles Barnett III.
p. cm.—(Graphic library. Disasters in history)
Summary: "In graphic novel format, tells the story of the Donner Party's struggle to reach California despite harsh weather and starvation"—Provided by publisher.
Includes bibliographical references and index.
ISBN-13: 978-0-7368-5479-5 (hardcover)
ISBN-10: 0-7368-5479-7 (hardcover)
ISBN-13: 978-0-7368-6874-7 (softcover pbk.)
ISBN-10: 0-7368-6874-7 (softcover pbk.)
1. Donner Party—Juvenile literature. 2. Pioneers—California—Biography—Juvenile literature. 3. Pioneers—West (U.S.)—Biography—Juvenile literature. 4. Overland journeys to the Pacific—Juvenile literature. 5. Frontier and pioneer life—West (U.S.)—Juvenile literature.
I. Frenz, Ron, ill. II. Barnett, Charles, III, ill. III. Title. IV. Series.
F868.N5W415 2006
978'.02 2 22 2005031301

Art Director
Jason Knudson

Graphic Designers
Bob Lentz and Thomas Emery

Production Artist
Alison Thiele

Storyboard Artist
Jason Knudson

Colorist
Benjamin Hunzeker

Editor
Christine Peterson

Editor's note: Direct quotations from primary sources are indicated by a yellow background.

Direct quotations appear on the following pages:

Page 4, from a letter written by Tamsen Donner dated May, 11, 1846 (http://members.aol.com/DanMRosen/donner/may46.htm).

Page 12, from *The Expedition of the Donner Party and its Tragic Fate* by Eliza P. Donner Houghton (Chicago: A. C. McClurg & Co., 1911).

Page 18, from Mary Graves' account of Forlorn Hope as published in *History of the Donner Party, A Tragedy of the Sierra* by C. F. McGlashan, (Stanford University, California: Stanford University Press, 1940).

Page 24, from a statement given by Donner Party rescuer Daniel Rhoads in 1873 (http://www.geocities.com/Heartland/Ranch/5417/GenReports/DanielR.htm#bancroft).

Printed in the United States 5946

Table of Contents

Chapter 1

Chasing a Dream. 4

Chapter 2

Hastings Cutoff 10

Chapter 3

Trapped in the Mountains 16

Chapter 4

A Last Hope 22

More about the Donner Party 28
Glossary 30
Internet Sites 30
Read More 31
Bibliography 31
Index 32

CHAPTER 1
CHASING A DREAM
In the 1840s, thousands of Americans left their homes and businesses in the east and headed west to California. In May 1846, a group of emigrants left Independence, Missouri, bound for California. Along the way, they were joined by more emigrants, forming a group of 87 people and 23 wagons. This group would become known as the Donner Party.
George Donner and his wife, Tamsen, had a large farm in Illinois. But they were attracted to the free land in California.
There's plenty of rich farmland in California.
I have no doubt it will be an advantage to our children and to us.
It'll take a lot of work to travel 1,600 miles before fall.

James Reed and his wife, Margaret, appeared to be the wealthiest family in the group. But Reed's business had failed.
California is our chance to start over, Margaret. It's a dream, I tell you.
I hope you're right, James.
Other families, like Jacob and Elizabeth Donner, hoped for a better life in California.
Life should be easier for us in California.
With some hard work, we should be able to make a go of it there.
ROCKY MOUNTAINS
INDEPENDENCE
SIERRA NEVADA
GREAT SALT LAKE
CALIFORNIA
The Donner Party would follow a trail of wagon tracks across prairies, deserts, and mountains. If all went as planned, they would reach California before snow made it impossible to cross the Sierra Nevada mountain range.

At first, traveling was easy. The trail followed rivers as it crossed the plains. There was water to drink and plenty of wild game to eat.
Virginia, what do you suppose California is like?
I'm not sure, Elitha. My father says it's warm and sunny there all the time.
Just ahead of the Donner Party, Lansford Hastings was telling other emigrants about a new, shorter route to California. But Hastings had never traveled his cutoff with wagons.
My cutoff is faster and easier than the usual trail. We're sure to be in California before winter.

After two months, the Donner Party had crossed Kansas and Nebraska territories.
In late June 1846, the Donner Party arrived in Fort Laramie, Wyoming. At the fort, Reed met a mountain man who had followed Hastings Cutoff.
We've been reading about a shortcut to California.
I just took the cutoff back from California. You'll never get your wagons through.
You'd be better off taking the old route.
The emigrants decided to rest at Fort Laramie.
We're wasting time resting here for two days. It's still a long way to California.
Yes, but if we overwork the oxen, we won't make it to California.

By July 19, Hastings Cutoff was on everyone's mind. After three months, the emigrants still had 1,000 miles of rough trail to cover before reaching California.
The cutoff will save us a month.
That would put us in California in seven weeks.
I don't know, Reed. This cutoff sounds too good to be true.
Don't worry. We can always turn back if the cutoff gets rough.
Later that night, the emigrants took a vote.
We must decide.
Do we follow the longer route to the north, or the cutoff to the south?
South!
Cutoff!
South!

On July 28, the Donner Party reached Fort Bridger, Wyoming, where they stopped to rest. But if they knew what was happening on Hastings Cutoff, they might have kept going.
Your shortcut is covered with nothing but rocks and trees.
We should have gone the other way.
Hastings rode back along the cutoff to warn other travelers.
We'll be lucky if the wagons make it through Weber Canyon. I hope others find this note before they get there.

CHAPTER 2
HASTINGS CUTOFF
After three days of rest at Fort Bridger, the Donner Party continued along the cutoff. They approached the last chance to turn north and take the traditional route to Oregon and California. At the crossroads, they found Hastings' note.
What's it say, Reed?
Weber Canyon is bad. Hastings doesn't know if we can get through.
We're wasting time. Go find Hastings so he can lead us through this canyon.
We'll find him, George.

Reed found Hastings, but he refused to lead the Donner Party through the canyon. Instead, he showed Reed a different route.
If you head farther south, you'll find a small canyon that's easier to cross.
But that's unbroken territory. We'll have to cut our own trail!
It's the only way.
The Donner Party worked for days to clear a trail through the small canyon.
On August 22, the Donner Party pulled the last wagons over the new rough trail. William Eddy believed their troubles were just beginning.
Get some rest, William.
How can I rest? We lost 10 days cutting that trail, Eleanor. And if I figure right, our food will run out before we reach California.

After another week of slow travel, the Donner Party rested in Salt Lake Valley.
We've spent three weeks on this cutoff.
And we've only covered 36 miles.
We can't turn back now.
Near the Great Salt Desert, the Donner Party found another note from Hastings.
Two days and two nights. Hard driving. Cross desert. Reach water.
Can we trust Hastings?
We have no choice, Eddy.
There was no food, water, or firewood in the desert.
We need to bring as much water as we can.
Make sure the oxen have plenty of food.

On August 31, the Donner Party entered the desert. The large wagons of the Donners and Reeds sank in the salt and sand.
We can't keep up.
The oxen are exhausted. They can't pull the wagons.
Five days later, the Donner Party stumbled out of the desert. Supplies were low. Charles Stanton had a plan.
We need food. I'll ride ahead to Sutter's Fort for supplies.
Very good, Stanton. We'll meet up with you along the trail.
As September ended, the Donner Party's troubles continued.
Indians raided again. Cattle are missing.
Look at those geese. They're flying south. Winter is coming fast.

Delays and rough trails put many of the emigrants on edge. They were frustrated and tired. On October 5, John Snyder tried to drive his wagon past the Reeds' wagon. The oxen became tangled.
Get up that hill you blasted animal!
Snyder! You're hurting my oxen!
You can't tell me what to do!
Stop!
Snyder died from a stab wound.
After Snyder died, others met to decide Reed's fate.
Reed must be punished. I say we hang him.
We can't! I say we banish him.
Reed, you must leave now.
I'll come back, Virginia. I promise.

After the loss of Snyder and Reed, the Donner Party approached the Forty-Mile Desert.
Why are we stopping, Papa?
Our oxen are tired. I'm burying some things to lighten their load. We'll come back for them later.
By October 15, they reached Truckee River, Nevada. Like many others, Franklin Graves and his family had little food left.
XXX
Look, Father! Stanton's back with food.
As they rested and ate from the fresh supplies, some people became worried about the snow showing on the mountaintops.
Don't worry. Men at the fort said snow doesn't block the mountain pass until November.
That gives us about a month. We should let the oxen rest.
We're wasting time. Even with fresh supplies, we won't have enough to get us through.

CHAPTER 3
TRAPPED IN THE MOUNTAINS
On October 31, a blizzard struck while the Donner Party was trying to cross the Sierra Nevada, a dangerous mountain range in eastern California.
The George and Jacob Donner families and a few others were delayed by a broken wagon. The blizzard trapped this group of 22 emigrants near a small creek.
I've never seen such a terrible storm!
I can't tell where we are.
We'll never catch the others. We have to make camp here.

Meanwhile, the rest of the Donner Party pushed toward the mountaintop. But the snow was too deep.
If we could just get over the summit, the traveling will be easier.
But shouldn't we wait here for the others?
There's no time. If we don't cross the summit soon, we'll be trapped.
We'll try again in the morning, with or without the others.
The storm continued all night. When the travelers set out the next morning, at least 5 feet of new snow covered parts of the summit.
I can't see the summit through all this snow.
We'll never make it across. We'll have to camp here for the winter.

The 59 emigrants at Truckee Lake needed shelters. Louis Keseberg and his wife Philipine struggled to build a small shack.
We need to get this shack finished before the next storm hits.
I hope these logs can stand up to the snow and winds.
Six miles away, the Donner families were also making camp.
Take the wagon covers to make our tent stronger.
Take these quilts too.
For the next six weeks, 81 emigrants of the Donner Party remained trapped in the mountains. Many of their animals got lost in the storms and were buried in the snow.
By mid-December, the emigrants had killed their remaining animals for food. Most people were weak, ill, and starving. One person had died from starvation.
The cries of hunger from my brothers and sisters are more than I can stand.
We have to go for help.

On December 16, a group of 15 volunteers decided to cross the mountain to get help.
I don't know how long this will take.
We can only spare enough food for six days. We need food for the others in camp.
The snowshoers tried to find their way through the mountains. On the second day, they crossed the summit. But by the sixth day, they were lost in the mountains.
Which way should we go?
We need to keep heading west.
The deep snow made traveling slow and dangerous.
HELP!
Hold on, Mary!
I'm so cold and hungry, Father.
I wish I had food to give you.

On Christmas Day, another blizzard struck. The snowshoers were forced to make camp.
We haven't eaten in two days.
I can't go any farther.
Two days later, three people died of starvation. The remaining snowshoers faced a difficult decision.
We need food. If we ate the dead, we all could live.
Cannibalism? Graves, are you crazy?
We have no other food. If we die, then so will the others back at the camps.
Although they discussed cannibalism, no one could go through with it.
Surely, there must be some other way.
Days passed with nothing to eat. Again, the emigrants discussed eating the dead.
Mary, you need food. I'm afraid you may have to eat human flesh to survive.
Father! I just can't.
You may have to. It's your only hope.

As December ended, the remaining snowshoers realized they had no other choice. They decided to eat the dead.
By January 1847, the snowshoers had been away from Truckee Lake for almost a month. Eight people had died along the way.
How far do you think we have left?
I don't know. I'm starting to believe there is no end to these mountains.
On January 18, the survivors found a small ranch, just outside the mountains.
What's happened to these poor people?
They're starving. Get them some food. Hurry!

CHAPTER 4
A LAST ROPE
Back at Truckee Lake, people were starving. By February 1847, 13 people had died. The others had no food. People ate animal hides, rugs, and shoes to survive.
This hide doesn't belong to you, Mrs. Reed.
But we gave that hide to you to make your shelter, Mrs. Breen.
Then it's ours now.
Without that hide, my children will starve!
My children are hungry, too.

At the other camp, the Donners were not doing any better. Four people had died of starvation. Others were ill and dying.
Not if we can help it, dear.
Mama, is Papa going to die too?
By February 1847, only 31 emigrants remained at Truckee Lake. The survivors prayed and hoped for relief.
Hurry, James. Hurry.

After the snowshoers arrived at the ranch, a relief party was formed to rescue the remaining members of the Donner Party. On February 18, 1847, the rescuers crossed the summit.
I see the camps!
Hello? Hello!!
Listen. I hear voices!
I hear them, Mrs. Breen. Look. Help has come at last!
Are you men from California? Or do you come from heaven?
Once in camp, the rescuers realized they could not take all the emigrants with them.
We don't have enough food for everyone.
Then we take only those who are able to travel.
On February 22, 1847, the first relief party left Truckee Lake with 23 emigrants. They arrived safely at Sutter's Fort.

While members of the Donner Party struggled to stay alive, James Reed was working on a plan. After arriving in California, Reed gathered men and supplies to lead a relief party into the mountains.
It's not much farther. They're camped near the lake.
I hope we're not too late.
On March 1, 1847, Reed and his group reached the camp sites.
Papa! I knew you would find us.
Reed soon left with 17 emigrants. Tamsen Donner decided to stay.
George is dying. How can I leave?
Then I wish you the best, Mrs. Donner.
By March 7, Reed's group was in danger. They had little food. Patrick Breen and his family were too weak to go on.
You should come with us, Breen. We need to keep moving.
It's too dangerous, Reed. We're going to wait here for another relief party.
Reed left with three others. They crossed the mountains safely.

Eleven emigrants, including the Breen family, made a camp in the mountains. Their fire burned through the snow, creating a deep pit where they lived.
We are trapped here without food until help arrives.
Three people have died already. More of us will die if we don't get help soon.
Stranded in the mountains with no food, the Breens were faced with a difficult decision.
There is one way we could all live. We may have to eat human meat.
We can't!
We have no other food. Either we eat the dead or we die.
I cannot believe it has come to this.
For three days, the emigrants lived in the snowy pit with nothing to eat but the dead. On March 12, rescuers arrived.

By March 19, a third relief party had come and gone at the other camps. Tamsen Donner again decided to stay with her husband. A few days later, George Donner died. Only two survivors remained.
Mrs. Donner, it's the only way. There's nothing left. If we eat human meat, we will live.
I would rather die than resort to such a gruesome act!
Then you are sealing your fate.
Days later, Tamsen Donner died of starvation.
By April 21, 1847, the last relief party reached the camp at Truckee Lake. They led the last survivor out of the mountains.
The Donner Party's long and terrible journey west was finally over.

More About the Donner Party

- The Donner Party consisted of 87 people and 23 wagons. Only 29 of the 87 people in the Donner Party were men, age 15 or older. The rest were women and children.

- In all, 41 people died during the Donner Party's journey to California. Thirty-six people died in the mountains during the winter. Of those who died, 32 were male and nine were female.

- When the snow buried the cattle in the mountains, the emigrants used poles with bent nails on the end to search the snow for them.

- Washoe Indians brought a small amount of roots to the Breen family while they were trapped in the mountains.

- The group of snowshoers later became known as the Forlorn Hope.

- Four relief parties went into the Sierra Nevada to rescue the Donner Party. Forlorn Hope survivors William Eddy and William Foster volunteered to join the third relief party that went to the Donner Party camps.

- After the Donner Party reached California, soldiers found the emigrants' campsites in the mountains. The soldiers found bodies in one cabin and buried them. They then burned the cabin.

- Parts of the Sierra Nevada have been renamed for the Donner Party. Truckee Lake is now called Donner Lake. The mountain summit is called Donner Summit. The rocky path over the summit is named Donner Pass.

- In 2004, scientists found the location of the Donner camp near Alder Creek. Scientists dug up objects including bits of china, jewelry, pieces of bone, and a cooking hearth. Scientists are testing the bones to see if they are animal or human.

- After she arrived in California, Virginia Reed wrote her cousin and offered this advice about traveling west: "Never take no cutoffs and hurry along as fast as you can."

GLOSSARY

banish (BAN-ish)—to send someone away from a place and order the person never to return

cannibalism (KAN-uh-buh-liz-uhm)—the act of a human eating human flesh

cutoff (KUHT-of)—a shorter route than the one usually taken

emigrants (EM-uh-grantz)—people who have left their homes in search of new ones

relief party (ri-LEEF PAR-tee)—a group of people who try to save trapped people

INTERNET SITES

FactHound offers a safe, fun way to find Internet sites related to this book. All of the sites on FactHound have been researched by our staff.

Here's how:

1. *Visit www.facthound.com*
2. Type in this special code **0736854797** for age-appropriate sites. Or enter a search word related to this book for a more general search.
3. Click on the **Fetch It** button.

FactHound will fetch the best sites for you!

READ MORE

Bryant, Jill. *Wagon Train.* Real Life Stories. Mankato, Minn.: Weigl, 2003.

Calabro, Marian. *The Perilous Journey of the Donner Party.* New York: Clarion, 1999.

Rau, Dana Meachen. *The Life on the Oregon Trail.* Daily Life. San Diego: Kidhaven Press, 2002.

Wachtel, Roger. *The Donner Party.* Cornerstones of Freedom. New York: Children's Press, 2003.

BIBLIOGRAPHY

Houghton, Eliza Donner. *The Expedition of the Donner Party and its Tragic Fate.* Chicago: A. C. McClurg & Co., 1911.

Johnson, Kristin. *New Light on the Donner Party.* (http://www.utahcrossroads.org/DonnerParty).

Johnson, Kristin. *Unfortunate Emigrants: Narratives of the Donner Party.* Logan, Utah: Utah State University Press, 1996.

McGlashan, C. F. *History of the Donner Party: A Tragedy of the Sierra.* Stanford, Calif.: Stanford University Press, 1940.

INDEX

animals, 7, 12, 13, 14, 15, 18, 28

Breen, Margaret, 22, 24, 26
Breen, Patrick, 25, 26

cannibalism, 20, 21, 26, 27

Donner, Elitha, 6
Donner, Elizabeth, 5
Donner, George, 4, 10, 13, 16, 23, 25, 27
Donner, Jacob, 5, 16
Donner, Tamsen, 4, 12, 23, 25, 27

Eddy, William, 11, 12, 28

food, 11, 12, 13, 15, 18, 19, 20, 21, 22, 24, 25, 26, 27, 28
Fort Bridger, 9, 10
Fort Laramie, 7
Forty-Mile Desert, 15

Graves, Franklin, 15, 19, 20
Graves, Mary, 15, 18, 19, 20
Great Salt Desert, 12–13

Hastings, Lansford, 6, 9, 10, 11, 12
Hastings Cutoff, 6, 7, 8, 9, 10, 12

Keseberg, Louis, 18, 27
Keseberg, Philipine, 18

Reed, James, 5, 7, 8, 10, 11, 12, 14, 15, 25
Reed, Margaret, 5, 22, 23, 24
Reed, Virginia, 6, 14, 29
relief parties, 24, 25, 26, 27, 28

Salt Lake Valley, 12
Sierra Nevada, 5, 16–21, 24–27, 28, 29
snowshoers, 19–21, 24, 28
Snyder, John, 14, 15
Stanton, Charles, 13, 15
summit, 17, 19, 24, 29
Sutter's Fort, 13, 24

Truckee Lake, 18, 21, 22, 23, 24, 27, 29
Truckee River, 15

weather, 5, 13, 15, 16, 17, 18, 20
Weber Canyon, 9, 10–11